Animal Offspring

Ducks and Their Ducklings

Revised Edition

by Margaret Hall

T0044780

CAPSTONE PRESS
a capstone imprint

Pebble Plus is published by Capstone Press,
1710 Roe Crest Drive,
North Mankato, Minnesota 56003
www.mycapstone.com

Copyright © 2018 by Capstone Press, a Capstone
imprint. All rights reserved. No part of this
publication may be reproduced in whole or in part,
or stored in a retrieval system, or transmitted in
any form or by any means, electronic, mechanical,
photocopying, recording, or otherwise, without
written permission of the publisher.

Library of Congress Cataloging-in-Publication Data
Names: Hall, Margaret, 1947- author. Title: Ducks
and their ducklings : a 4D book / by Margaret Hall.
Description: Revised edition. | North Mankato,
Minnesota : Capstone Press, a Capstone imprint,
[2018] | Series: Pebble plus. Animal offspring |
Audience: Ages 4-8. | Includes bibliographical
references and index. Identifiers: LCCN 2017037871
(print) | LCCN 2017053188 (ebook) | ISBN
9781543508635 (eBook PDF) | ISBN 9781543508239
(hardcover) | ISBN 9781543508352 (pbk.) Subjects:
LCSH: Ducklings--Juvenile literature. | Ducks--
Juvenile literature. Classification: LCC SF505.3 (ebook)
| LCC SF505.3 .H36 2018 (print) | DDC 636.5/97--dc23
LC record available at https://
lccn.loc.gov/2017037871

Editorial Credits
Gina Kammer, editor; Sarah Bennett, designer;
Morgan Walters, media researcher;
Katy LaVigne, production specialist

Photo Credits
Shutterstock: Africa Studio, 15, right 20, Anna
Semenova, 3, Anneka, 13, left 20, Dave Doe, 17, Edwin
Butter, Cover, Gumpanat, right 21, Menno Schaefer,
7, Nick Starichenko, left 21, Tom Franks, 19, Travkin
Igor, 5, yaibuabann, 11, Yakov Oskanov, 9

Note to Parents and Teachers

The Animal Offspring set supports national science
standards related to life sciences. This book describes
and illustrates ducks and their ducklings. The images
support early readers in understanding the text.
The repetition of words and phrases helps early
readers learn new words. This book also introduces
early readers to subject-specific vocabulary words,
which are defined in the Glossary section. Early
readers may need assistance to read some words and
to use the Table of Contents, Glossary, Read More,
Internet Sites, Critical Thinking Questions, and Index
sections of the book.

Printed in the United States   5979

Table of Contents

Ducks

Ducks are birds
with strong bills
and webbed feet.
Young ducks are
called ducklings.

Ducks and their ducklings

live near lakes and ponds.

A female is a duck.

Sometimes a female

is called a hen.

A male is a drake.

Drakes and ducks mate.

hen

drake

Laying Eggs

Most ducks lay 4 to 12 eggs.

A duck sits on her eggs

to keep them warm.

Ducklings

Ducklings hatch after about one month. A duckling breaks the egg open with its egg tooth.

egg tooth

Ducklings have soft feathers called down. Ducklings will grow new feathers after two months.

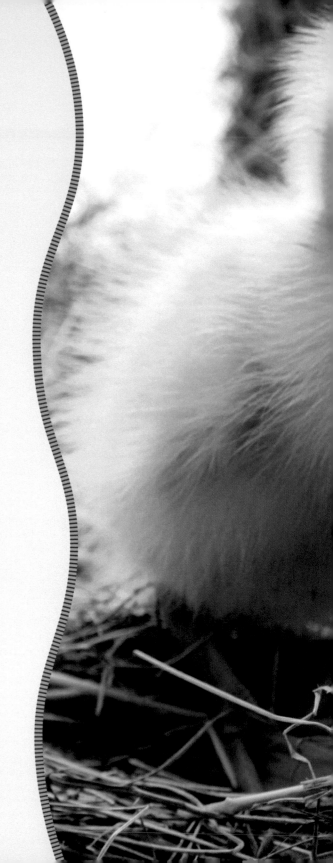

Growing Up

Ducklings follow their mother to the water. She teaches them to swim and to dive.

Ducklings become adults.

Drakes and ducks fly.

Watch Ducks Grow

hatching

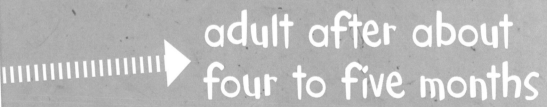

adult after about
four to five months

21

Glossary

bill—the hard part of a bird's mouth; ducks use their bills to peck at food; bills also are called beaks

bird—a warm-blooded animal with wings, two legs, and feathers; birds lay eggs; most birds can fly

egg tooth—a tooth-like part that sticks out on a duckling's bill; the egg tooth falls off shortly after the duckling hatches

feather—one of the light, fluffy parts that covers the skin on a bird's body; ducks have waterproof feathers

hatch—to break out of an egg; ducklings hatch from their eggs after about one month

mate—to join together to produce young

webbed—having folded skin or tissue between an animal's toes or fingers; ducks have webbed feet to help them swim better

Read More

Delano, Marfe Ferguson. *Ducklings.* Explore My World. Washington, D.C.: National Geographic Kids, 2017.

Hasselius, Michelle. *Ducks.* Farm Animals. North Mankato, Minn.: Capstone Press, 2017.

Mitchem, James. *Farm Animals.* New York: DK Publishing, 2016.

Internet Sites

Use FactHound to find Internet sites related to this book.

Visit *www.facthound.com*

Just type **9781543508239** and go.

Critical Thinking Questions

1. What things do ducklings learn from their mother?

2. Ducks are described as having webbed feet. What does "webbed" mean?

3. How do ducklings hatch?

Index